Also by Carlton D. Fisher

Silhouette of a Man

AND THE MOON IS FULL TONIGHT

New and Selected Poems by
Carlton D. Fisher

JANE'S BOY PRESS
Watertown, NY
www.janesboypress.com

Jane's Boy Press
219 Arlington Street
Watertown, NY 13601

www.janesboypress.com

First Jane's Boy Press Edition, October 2014

for work,
for family,
for men and boys,
and for all the other things
that keep me awake at night

TABLE OF CONTENTS

What must it mean
to only be visible
as a reflection of the sun?

The Moon Rises for Allan

I have watched the full moon arch
over the waters of Lake Ontario
and considered that I may never be loved again,
not under the terms I wish to be loved,
that maybe the demands I place on love
are such that no one could ever meet them,
that I have lost the power I once had
to inspire devotion or adoration
with the ease I always could.

And I wonder,
did I force love away from me,
reject it one too many times,
that I will never be seen as an object of affection?
In his eyes, I don't know what I am,
maybe a monster that wants to feed on youth,
maybe just some old man he will never be,
maybe just some regret he will catalogue
with other things he wishes he had left undone.

But in him I see the boy I was,
and I want to give him the life I didn't have,
then open his eyes to the wonder and possibilities
of the glorious time that spreads out before him,
time enough to conquer the world
if he only lets the possibility of the act
be something that he will consider.

He said, in French,
he keeps hoping for something
like love at first sight
but ducks and covers at the real possibility,
maybe because of the source,
or maybe because
he hunts it like we hunt the Fountain of Youth,
wishing we could find it,
but secretly believing it's just a myth,
this man just crossed over the threshold
between the new adult world
and the boyhood that oppressed him,
afraid even of the blood that fills his body,
unaware of the beauty that is not only on his skin,
but alive in the soul he struggles to conceal,
but only reveals that much more clearly.

But what do I have to offer
beyond words he's unwilling to believe?

Above Lake Ontario,
the moon is full tonight,
bloated unto bursting,
like my heart, clogged with a love
that has no target to receive it,
feeling the pressure inside my chest building up,
sure that it will,
in the end,
simply explode and destroy me.

If I was better at love,
I would know how to make him see
that what he wants is right here
if only he was willing to accept it.
It seeps from the scars and craters
of the others who have crashed into this heart,
made their mark and disintegrated,
and it seems he's one more shadow on the moon
that will pass across it and disappear,
turn out only to be a cloud at midnight
burning into the afterimage
of the heavenly body
I have stared at too long.

How I Lost my Vanilla Ice T-shirt

It was April
1991
and I was cool
because I loved Vanilla Ice.

And so what if I was in Model UN
and liked speech & debate
and was more interested in dinosaurs
than dating?
I liked Vanilla Ice—
to the extreme.

So that night
I was going to the dance,
and my mom was coming with me
to chaperone.
Because I was cool—
cool as Ice.

Now let's remember,
I was cool.
And anybody who's cool knows
you have to be careful
when going with your parent
to a school function.
So I was happy
when my mom
asked to borrow my t-shirt,
and I could see
Vanilla Ice
glowering in a tough guy stance
from the front of her chest—
Vanilla Ice, Ice Baby.

And so
that night
while the Beach Boys
were Surfin' USA,
and my mom was dancing on the floor
with the teachers she could coax out,
she leaned to me and said,
"I'm going to get a drink of water."

And then she fell.
I was on the stairs by the stage
in the school gymnasium

and she was on the floor—
brown slacks
Vanilla Ice T-shirt
and the strangest stare on her face
as she looked straight at the ceiling,
one leg stiff.

When they wheeled the gurney
from the gym,
Becky said, "Everything will be alright."
But I knew better
because I got an "A" in Health class,
and so I remembered
that you never do CPR
on someone who's alive

I got to make the call
to tell my grandma that my mother had fallen down.

And then I made the call
to my father to say, "She fell."

And then we went to the ER
where they have the tiny room—
the room away from the waiting room.
We waited.
And when the staff came in
it was like choreography—
like a dance—
the way they each zeroed in
on their charge.
And Cory's mom
(who wasn't at the dance
because she was on duty)
told me she was sorry.

And I could hear my grandma crying.

And later
when I was on the phone
in one of the empty rooms,
telling Mr. Francey from Guidance
that I could get a job,
that I could cook the meals,
that I could shop for groceries on weekends,
I saw my dad walk down the hall.

Years later he told me
what she looked like on the table:
blue
dead
blue
opened
blue
covered.
But not my mom.

They had cut open her chest
and tried to massage her heart,
tried to make it work again.
But it had made the decision to stop
and it was firm in that decision.

That's how I lost my Vanilla Ice t-shirt.

BONDS

My mom loved the old Bond movies—
Connery or Moore, all European swagger
and masculine insistence,
martinis shaken, not stirred.
She'd watch old VHS tapes of them with my grandfather
on Sunday mornings
while Grandma and I were in the kitchen
and Dad slept in the living room recliner.

My father slept through a lot of family events—
weekends, holidays,
early evenings.
On weekends, we visited my grandparents on both sides,
but during the week
we were alone on the farm.
Mom hadn't married a farmer.
She married an Agway salesman with a Master's degree
who was waiting for a teaching job,
and then he was a college prof in the ag department
at the local two-year school,
but he'd stopped being the man she met long before that.

My father has a certain charm he can use in courtship.
I watched it pull my stepmother in.
He knows how to be funny and playful when he needs to be.
But my mom learned that, after the "I dos,"
that more or less ends,
and he's moody, sullen, distant,
focused on what he wants and not much else.

And somehow, along the way,
she became a farmer's wife—
my dad's great dream of a family farm,
like his grandfather had owned,
like my grandfather had escaped.
She became fluent in the language
of the infected cow,
who scrambles and kicks when you wash her teat,
the butt and thump of the hungry calf,
who will ram the bottle into you, thinking the milk will flow faster,
and the silent, sullen dinner,
where her husband shoveled food into his mouth,
left his dirty plates at his place at the table,
and went to bed after watching the news.

She told me once,
that she really married him
because she was afraid no one else would ask—
that the first time she thought about divorce
was a week after the wedding,
when she was walking alone beside the road
because my dad was travelling for sales,
that she had made a mistake in ever trusting him,
believing the man she had met
was the one she had married.

My mother taught me
you can never trust a man,
and my father illustrated
the lessons she imparted.

I find myself always wary,
certain I can't trust the men in my life,
keeping them at a certain distance,
where I can examine each thing they say,
hold it up to the light to find the lie inside of it,
use the spy's games of perception
to suss out where the real threat is—
all of the cautions and conditions I learned from my mother,
whom love had left shaken, not stirred.

DISTEMPER

She said it was the humane thing to do,
and I didn't know there were more humane ways
that we couldn't afford,
especially for just a barn cat,
so I filled the bucket with water,
and tried to get the temperature just right
so it would be like a warm bath—
not scalding like the one his mother had fallen into
when she was a kitten,
burning off half her fur and healing her nipples over
so that he was the only one to survive
out of the litter of eight.

And once it was bath temperature,
I picked Buddy up,
with his one clubbed paw
that had gotten caught
in the gutter cleaner chain, but healed,
and I lowered him into the bucket,
because my mom said it was the humane thing to do,
because if you don't stop distemper
it will spread to all the cats,
and they will all get lethargic and quiet
and sniffle and slowly, slowly
just stop living,
but it will be painful and awful and long.

And I watched, as he twitched a little bit,
not thinking, at eight ,
that the water was filling his lungs,
that this wasn't like just softly going to sleep,
but the distemper had made him too weak to do much more
than flinch a little bit beneath the surface,
wouldn't even allow him to lift his head above the water,
and when it was over,
I pulled him out of the bucket
and laid him on the towel—
Buddy, who was just a barn cat,
like every other barn cat,
each one of which I had a name for
had held from the day they were born,
had watched as they opened their eyes
and went from dragging their fat kitten bellies
along the bottoms of boxes
to running between the dandelions on warmer spring days.

I wrapped the towel over him,
and left him for my father
who would spread him on the field
like other things we no longer had use for,
not thinking, at eight,
that the coy dogs would come
and drag the body off.

I did it because my mother asked,
because she said it was the humane thing to do.

Dark Side of the Moon

The moon hides the secrets of the dead
on her dark side.
This is why we don't land there anymore.
The news that came back was dire:

That your mother was crying in all her wedding photos
because she knew she was making a mistake,
that her joy at your birth
was tempered by the knowledge
that your existence was like a leash,
binding her to your father forever.

Einstein's greatest wish
was that he could take back the bomb,
give back all the lives
he had unwittingly been the accessory in taking,
but once a force like that is out of its cage
it never can be put back in.

Diana guards the secrets of the dead,
the secrets I know as well,
the ones my mother told me,
the ones I hide from my brother,
whose only memories of our mother
are the ones that I have given him.
"She's crying because she was happy,"
I say,
and remind him he was a miracle,
not another chain
binding her to the black hole of my father's insanity.

I am the dark side of the moon,
the keeper of secrets that never should have been told.

MISSED CONNECTIONS

March 4th:
"You were driving a red truck,
and you turned without your signal on,
but you saw me on the corner,
and I thought you smiled.
If you did, hit me up
you made me smile too."

March 10th:
"You were jogging in the rain
at the entrance to the park
while I was walking my dog.
You said hello,
and I just didn't know what to say.
You were so beautiful.
Please tell me you saw me too."

March 16th:
"You were looking for the right kind of chips,
And I helped you find them.
Your eyes were so deep I didn't know
how to tell you what I really wanted to,
but I'm saying it now.
If you're reading.
I can't stop thinking of you."

All these moments of lives touching,
glancing off one another.
If I could post my own
it would say:

April 2nd:
"You were walking out the door,
and I was screaming that all I wanted
was for you to go.
But that wasn't what I meant,
and I thought you of all people would know that.
And by time I meant to say I was sorry,
you were too far away to hear."

If you're reading,
I mean it now.

SCARIFICATION

Despite stereotypes,
if they sit together long enough,
even gay men will discuss their scars.
In a show and tell of injury,
we'll pull up our shirt sleeves,
roll up pant legs,
point to memories that have left their marks.

I can list mine easily:
here is the one from falling in the driveway
when I was two
and getting a pebble stuck in my head
(the scar, by the way, the doctor assured my parents
would disappear in six months or less);
here is where I fell off my bike
while trying to get into shape;
here is where I took extreme measures
getting rid of a pimple
and left a permanent mark
that looks like a pimple;
here is where my grandmother's cat
taught me about keeping my distance.

(I don't show the hernia scar
unless we've had too much to drink
or I am looking for an excuse
to undo my pants.)

My friends have scars less frivolous.

"This is the scar
where the soldier dragged me out of the barracks
by my hair and tore my scalp
when he found out his roommate and I
were more than just friends."

"This is where my father hit me
with the rock
when I told him I was gay."

"This line is where he cut me
when I told him that I loved him
and he called me a fag."

We show the scars
that illustrate our histories,
but we don't talk about the ones inside—
the ones that are invisible
unless you get close enough;
then you can even see those too.

Tarot Reading

I've asked every card
in every deck
and they keep giving me the same answer--
that I will never be with you.

You will love him,
and if not him
then another him,
but not me.

I've tried standing on the sidelines,
and I've tried quitting the game,
but neither option has worked,
and so I guess I'll watch.

Finding the will to move on
can be like finding the reason
to get out of bed on a winter morning.

I know I need to do it,
but it's just so cold.

POLICE LINE

You want so badly to leave that place behind,
the physical and the mental one,
but you can turn your back on a room,
run miles away from it,
and still never leave it.

You're not supposed to blame yourself—
that's what they always say—
but you were taught better lessons than that:
don't take rides from strangers,
don't let them into your room,
don't let yourself get caught in that moment
where no is only a suggestion he feels he can ignore,
and so you don't blame yourself
except for when you do,
which is all the time.

That first time,
I sat up all night at the foot of the bed
while he just slept there in my space
and I waited for him to leave,
reading *Hannibal Lecter, My Father* by Kathy Acker
because it was the first book
I could put my hands on
and there was nowhere else to go in that small space,
that single dorm room that barely fit a bed and desk
and nowhere to send that truth to
when I told the RA and he laughed like it was a joke
because the story was miscast, wasn't it?
Because it never happens to men—
the fingers where they don't belong,
the mouth forced to be where you didn't want it to go,
the threat that if you scream
there's a gun outside in the car,
so isn't it easier for everyone
if you just pretend you meant yes?

And even when he leaves,
there's knowing he knows where you live,
that he can come and find you again,
and the night that he does—
that he did—
I was thankful for the one friend I had who knew
who came by and made my excuses to leave.

Why is it so much harder
to tell this story as "I,"
so much more preferable to leave it "you,"
to distance myself from the scene of the crime?

And because I didn't say more,
didn't speak up to people I could make listen,
he did it again—to a woman that time—
on his own campus,
and all he got was expelled
while I had nightmares for months
and couldn't be touched without wanting to scream.

Everything heals eventually
and scars become good armor
until someone peels them off—
this time the uncle who vowed friendship and safety
and waited until I was asleep
to become hungry mouth and pressing fingers—
the salt of his dry skin burning inside my asshole
as he worked me over in his mouth
and I said "no, no, no" so quietly
to keep from waking the family,
to keep from getting him in trouble,
and when he was done with me
he whispered in my ear,
"You're pretty hard to resist,"
like I was a tray of fine chocolate
luring him off his diet.

And when I worried about the way he looked at my brothers,
thought about what he had done to me at twenty-four
and what he might do to someone younger,
I told,
with all the hurt and pain and burning of it,
I told,
and for a brief time there was understanding
before my family decided I had simply "confused" him—
like some fog that came down and clouded his visibility,
made "no:" into a foreign language
incomprehensible despite being almost universal.

And I let that be their story
because it was easier for them,
easier for me if I wanted to belong,
but I couldn't stay,
put that place to my back
and those people behind me

and still I cannot get out of those moments.

My body is a crime scene—
the kind of place the neighbors avoid,
where the trash blows up against the fence
and the needles gather beneath the leaves.
I should be wrapped in yellow tape
and declared off limits—
which is what I've done in so many ways.
I can't trust someone who will touch me,
no matter how badly I want to be touched,
can't believe someone can love me
no matter how open his heart.

I am the wrong side of town,
the other side of the tracks,
the dark end of the street,
the one place in the world
where it's impossible to believe
that anything can come to any good.
I am where lightning has struck twice
and burned what was good to the ground,
and eventually even fools learn
not to build in that part of town.

Spell Book

Lately, I find myself looking for an incantation
that would wipe away the last four years
and allow me to change my mind.

What is the Latin word for,
"please let time melt and fold over"?
And if I get it wrong again,
how many times can I say it?

What is the word for, "I changed the locks behind you
when I should have blocked the door
so you couldn't leave"?

In my picture of that morning,
I see so clearly how it could have been
if for once I'd held my tongue
and held you
and told you not to worry,
showed you that you didn't need to.

What are the words that calm the hurt of knowing
that I didn't just love you and let you go,
but that I pushed and kicked and screamed over you
rather than listen and let you come back?

That I once held love and crushed it
when my hands now ache to be full?

Soma Cube

A new lover's body
is a puzzle to be unlocked—
finding the switches and pressure points
that turn the temple fires
from faint glow to blaze.

Which inch of the neckline
is the one that makes his muscles slack,
makes his head roll back on a pivot,
exposes his throat to you
as though he were offering himself up
to the wolf, the vampire,
to anything that would make that sensation
come alive?

What is the best method
for navigating the curve of his sides?
Would your lips make him whimper softly
like the small voice of a man
weak and alone in the dark,
or would it take the strong touch of your hands,
grasping along the soft, rarely touched plains
of his tight belly?

When you kneel between his spread legs,
will he curl like a leaf before you,
protecting his soft center,
or will he spread wider,
rise up to meet you,
offer you entry if it's something you crave?

And when he releases
and lies limp in sheets,
chest slicked with the sweet aftermath
of what your body has wrought on his,
will he remember you are there,
reach out for you,
let his hands find their way along your body?
Or will you lie beside him,
your purpose served,
his puzzle solved,
and your interest already fading,
thinking about something new—
maybe the taste of the wine from dinner,
maybe the first time, when you thought this was love?

BALLAD OF THE LONELY HEART

Love is the thin sliver of glass
that pierces your chest
as you stare at his back as he is leaving,
the room a shambles of your anger,
the moment burned into your retina
so deeply
you will always be able to see it—
the hitch in his shoulders that may have been a sob,
the moment the door catches
that may have been a pause,
a second of reconsideration.

Love is the silence on the stairs
after the door clicks shut,
the cold puff of night breeze
that reaches your face where you have stopped,
the last words dying on your tongue
before you've had a chance to consider
if they were, "Don't leave,"
or something to send him further away.
That breath of night,
more than the click of the latch,
is what makes you certain
that this time he is really gone.

In all my life,
all love has taught me
is that I can never be enough for anyone,
least of all myself.

THE ORIGIN OF THE MOON

The article says billions of years ago
the moon wandered alone,
possessed by its own momentum
until it collided with Earth,
its core ripped from it to join ours,
losing the heart of itself
to a foreign planet,
and taking some of the dust with it
pulling back, but caught in orbit.

And since then it has gravitated
to the world it lost its very center to,
never able to leave,
grasping only the soft pieces
that the planet no longer misses
as it floats in and out of its shadows.

No matter how hard I try,
I can't help thinking of you.

BOOMERANG

You said that first time you were flirting.
It was a safe thing to do—
throwing it out there in your office
with people in and out
and my boyfriend standing next to me,
safe to know it could be put out there
without it coming back to you,
not knowing it wasn't the only time you'd see me.

The next time was without safety nets—
me uncoupled, you in a crowd,
but not one where you needed to be professional—
the first time we were peers.
Strange how some things can loop back
even after a very long time.
But you reached your hand up to catch it anyway.

At what point could this cycle have been broken?
I've looked and looked for the perforation
along which it could be torn,
but it always seems to come around again—
this feeling that should have ended
when you told me the brief moment we had
was more than you thought you wanted.

And yet so many of my sleepless nights are because of you
that I have learned to trace the outline of your profile
in the relief of the ceiling above my bed.

In a time so long
that I have forgotten the names of some of the men
who have come between then and now,
I can still play out every detail in my mind
of every moment we spent together,
and I can't find the poison capsule inside them
that makes them taste bitter enough
to stop me from turning them over and over again in my mouth,
longing for the point at which they were fresh,
but settling for the stale memory in the absence of anything new.

I've tried friendship.
I've tried hating you.
I've tried imposed silence that weighed on me more heavily
than any unmet desire ever could,
and still after over ten years
of learning I would never find gold in this darkness,

I spin and spin in the air between us,
waiting for you to catch me again,
while you've built a completely different life
that still doesn't have room for me in it.

Still I throw again and again,
waiting for it to come back to me
the way what you once threw so casually
came back to you and has never left.

Dark Animal

a black dog
is a manifestation
an omen
marking a place of tragedy
warning of tragedy to come

She told me there was nothing there,
would reach around the doorframe
and flick the old light switch that clicked,
echoing off the plaster walls of the empty room,
the space in front of my dresser now empty.

But I had seen Him.

And when the lights were off
and she had gone to sleep,
He came in the night and stood over my bed,
hot breath and smell of livestock
leaning in close to me,
kissing my hand or pulling back the covers,
lifting me in charcoal paws
the claws dangerous enough to tell me
this was a moment of silence.

I learned not to scream.

Decades later,
after my mother had died,
after that home has disintegrated and crumbled,
and after the night my step mother called
to tell me there was a giant black dog
standing in the middle of her living room
I read about Him,
learned what He was
or what He might be—
protector,
destroyer,
harbinger.

Cold lips on an infant's small hand.

Even after all these times,
even in these words spreading across the page,
sometimes it feels like He's looking,
reaching out from that old empty farmhouse
where no one lives anymore,

passing His fingers through the years I have used
to distance myself from that place,
grasping for the body on which He left his mark
before I had even left my crib.

He knows about the others.

One of these nights,
there will be a noise on the stairs,
and when I step into the hallway,
He'll be there to remind me
that the marked don't escape.
They may run into adulthood,
build knowledge like daylight that burns
through the things they saw at night with child eyes,
but those things can run fast,
and they don't need to stop,
and they do catch up
some night
when you're alone.

And they don't need to be seen to be real.

DRINK OF WATER

You said,
"I'm going to get a drink of water,"
and never came back.

I said, "OK,"
and that's the last thing
I ever said to you that I know you heard.

You said,
"I'm going to get a drink of water,"
and wandered away
and everything seemed fine,
as it should have been.
I remember looking at you walking away,
chocolate colored slacks
and my Vanilla Ice t-shirt,
and try to remember
if there was a sign,
but you were just going for a drink of water,
so I didn't pay enough attention
to discover nuance,
to have seen something different,
and from what the doctors said,
it wouldn't have mattered if i did
because it was probably too late
a few weeks before then
but I still examine that moment
and wonder what I should have seen
and think if I had known then
but I didn't,
and so you went to get a drink of water.

It's hot at school dances,
and we couldn't wear shoes
because the school said the sneakers
would scuff up the gym floor,
but after that night they let us wear shoes
because at first we thought you had slipped
and hit your head
on the way to get a drink of water
and so that is part of your legacy--
that Lisbon students can wear shoes at dances
even though you didn't slip before you fell.

The water fountain isn't there anymore,
in the corner of the gymnasium,

because the gymnasium isn't there anymore.
They turned it into an auditorium
like you always wanted
for when you were directing
the school talent shows,
and people no longer get up during performances
to get a drink of water
from the corner in front of the stage
as they did then,
because there is no fountain to drink from.
When they showed me the auditorium
when i went back for the 10-year reunion,
I looked from the doors at the back, but would not go in
because I knew
no matter how much the room had changed
that I would see you there.

You went to get a drink of water
and then someone said you fell
and I ran to that corner
leaned up against the steps,
didn't do any of the heroic things
a good son ought to do.
I just saw you with one stiff leg
elevated off the floor
and the way you stared up at the gymnasium ceiling,
and though someone took my hand
and led me away
I am forever in that moment on the stairs,
staring at you not looking at me,
calling out for you,
but the doctors say you were gone even then,
10 feet away from the fountain,
in the darkened gym,
thirsty and tired
and not able to get that drink of water.

LIZ PHAIR IN EXILE

Liz Phair told *Spin Magazine*
that she would rather be beautiful than smart,
and my heart broke a little
to think of all the times I had cranked *Exile in Guyville*
on my car stereo
and screamed along to "Fuck and Run" and "Divorce Song,"
the number of times I had managed to quote her lyrics
in undergraduate papers for gender studies classes
and celebrated her low-fi, home-demo
jeans-and-t-shirt sexuality
that refused to bow down and beg to be pretty,
that more often than not
refused to preface, "fuck you"
with "I want to."

I wanted my Liz back,
who could play a guitar like Keith Richards
and sang tunelessly but honestly.

But Liz had gotten a makeover,
blow-dried and feathered her hair,
wore lace without irony and peek-a-boo fuck pants,
and wrote songs with Britney Spears' old producer
where she sang about being "Extraordinary"
but seemed anything but
as she was begging for a guy's attention,
harmonizing with the layered backing track.

Liz had given me hope
that you could be powerful on your own—
alone but not lonely,
and now all she wanted to do was sing about boys,
and even when she sang something kind of dirty,
it was begging for a man
to treat her like a porn star.

I'd watched my mother bend then break
under the weight of a bad man
because she had been told that you were nothing
if you weren't married,
wanted, even though she was dead,
to go to her grave,
press the speakers of my boombox against the ground,
and play "Johnny Sunshine," where a man took Liz for everything
but she won out in the end,
wanted to play "6'2""

and let her know she was always so much bigger
than she gave herself credit for.

But I put Liz away on a shelf
and moved on to other things,
realizing that legends may always have the ring of truth,
but some people will never believe them.

The Lycanthrope's Dream

When we dream
we dream of the moon--
how she calls to us,
entreats us to obey her.
In the shadow-speckled night of the forest
we are her children,
she our master.
We run.

You who do not know
the thrill of the kill,
the feel of the flesh breaking
between the teeth,
cannot know the release
that comes
with blood letting

the orgiastic thrill
of the consumption of life.

By day we walk among you,
uncomfortable in these hairless skins.
You see us shy away.
In this form, we are at our weakest.
In this form, you are at your most brutal.

You have made the mistake
of assuming
we are men
who become wolves by night,
when what we are is wolves
who become men by day.

Our savagery by shadow,
our kinship with the darkness,
is simply our will to survive.
But we never seem to understand
those among you
who can practice your predation by day--
the men who are men,
the monsters upon two legs.

Romance Novels

My mother always woke up
hours before she needed to,
because my father was a slow riser,
and she had to speak to him repeatedly
to get him to wake up to milk the cows,

Unless she did it alone.

She sat under the yellowed light in our kitchen
reading romance novels at two in the morning,
drinking her coffee,
going into the bedroom every ten minutes,
saying, "David, it's time to get up."
My father would roll over,
say in his sleep, "C'mon, let's go
        gotta get up, c'mon
        we need to get going."

As though he was the one waiting

She would go back to her coffee—
his living snooze alarm—
Working her way through
Danielle Steele, Victoria Holt, Erica Jong.
If she was alive now,
I imagine she would be an acolyte
of Nicholas Sparks, Nora Roberts,
and bodice rippers
where women with heaving bosoms
barely contained by their too-tight corsets
sought solace in the embrace
of a half naked man
at the base of a waterfall
or in front of a field of wild horses.

My mother slept at the very edge of their bed,
precariously balanced on the verge of tipping into oblivion—
the farthest point she could get from my father
without sleeping in another room.

She told me once that she married him
only because she thought no one else would ask,
first considered divorce
the week they returned from their honeymoon.

I still see her at that table,
reading romance novels,
trying to find the heat of passion
in the winter of her marriage.

ROMANTIC COMEDY

Last night,
after a week of partial nights,
I finally slept
and dreamt you loved me.

We were lost in an amusement park.
You were separated from your boyfriend,
and through a series of unlikely events
you learned to love me.

And at the end, I was holding you
like I held you that one night
before you decided it was more
than what you wanted.

And then it turned out
it was actually a movie we were in
that I had written—
and after the happy ending
you went back to him.

Even in my dreams,
the only way I can see you loving me
is still only pretend.

SPIDER MEDICINE

Let me cocoon inside you,
like the caterpillar wrapped in silk,
waiting for the spring thaw to warm it again,
so it can break free and spread its wings
to embrace the hot summer to come.

Let me wrap the strands of your spinnerets
around my middle,
and blanket myself in the security
of the space beside you
that you call your home,
so that I may sleep and dream of becoming,
metamorphose into beauty unrelated
to the plain thing you have always seen.

Let me hide in pupal darkness
where you won't see the changes
until I can emerge as the thing of beauty
that you have never thought me to be,
golden and wet in early morning light,
new skin and color at first blinding
in its brilliance, so you shade your eyes
in wonder that something so illuminated
could have risen from the body
of that dull, uninteresting thing
you always saw in my place.

Let me cocoon inside you,
bent on becoming that which you cannot resist,
and let my transformation be the beginning
of my gift to you,
as I renounce every bit of my being,
to be what you always wanted.

Let it be the cocoon in which I can become,
and not the swathing bands of gossamer
with which you will wrap me to feed.

CONSIDER THE MOON

What must it mean
to only be visible
as a reflection of the sun?
What is the depth of loneliness
hanging in the night sky,
knowing that you are only seen
because of the light of something else,
when you have kept the entire world
as the center of your orbit,
and yet it only sees you
because of another heavenly body
it revolves around?

Consider what it means,
to lift and release the tides
and still not generate a warmth,
to be able to disappear entire nights
and not impact anything?
No wonder the moon makes us crazy.
Sometimes we resort to whatever we can
if it means the ones at the centers of our lives
will notice us, even if only briefly.

I think of you,
on moonlit nights,
and how I miss the pull of your gravity,
but I've turned my dark side toward you now.
I deserve to be more than a reflection.

THE NEW MATTRESS

When I bought the new mattress
I took the old one and put it in what I decided would be the guest room,
though I don't usually have any guests.
As I moved it there, I thought of the history that it had
in its stains and markings, the lives that had been lived-on it.

The ex-boyfriend who revealed one morning that, at 31,
he was still occasionally a bed wetter, and how I tried to appear fine
even though I was soaked in piss,
how it soaked the sheets and the pillow top,
and I had to pull the steam cleaner out and do my best
to erase that stain, and even after it was gone,
I still flipped the mattress over, disgusted and still feeling filthy,
even though I reassured him that everything was fine.

The night I had spent barely sleeping on the very edge of the bed,
afraid the man I slept with would wake up in another fury,
add to the damage he had already exacted on my body,
the sore bruises that were developing one by one,
the ring around my upper arm and the footprint on my chest,
all because I had told him he had had enough to drink.

The nights I had spent awake with the phone next to my head,
the cord stretching from the living room into the bedroom of my old apartment,
waiting, hoping, that my grad school boyfriend would call,
knowing all the time that he was with his ex-boyfriend,
and knowing what it meant when he didn't call, that I was as always,
second place in his life.

But I remembered the love that had played out across the surface of it as well,
the tears of joy and sometimes ecstasy, the occasional moments when I had cum so hard
that the room had spun and I had collapsed back onto it, shaken but happy,
the nights I had fallen asleep beside someone I loved, holding him as he breathed,
drifting off to the sound of each exhale, hoping that was the moment I could live inside of
for something like the rest of my life.

In two years, since I bought the new one, no one has stayed over with me.
slept beside me on the firm new surface of the memory foam,
made me think that there was some sort of love that would endure.
When I change the sheets now, I notice that only one side has any wear,
that the other side looks factory-fresh, the way it did the day the plastic wrap came off,
and I think how maybe there will never be anyone who stays the night again,
how the nights stretch out before me, one by one and silent,
with only the sound of my dog's snoring to break the monotony
of this room in which I seem to forever be alone.

Grammar Lesson

You have taught me
in your second person
I am past tense,
was briefly future conditional,

that even though I have revised our story
to place you in past perfect
I can never hope
to return to present tense.

It is what I deserve.
I know I can never be enough
no matter what you might mean to me,
no matter how I might try to say it.

I am lost in your revision lines
as you move on to better things
and I am left here remembering you,
knowing I will always speak in singular.

DUSTED

I am
so easy
to leave
behind.

Like a paperback,
read cover to cover,
its secrets revealed,
laying on the bench
in the waiting area
of the bus station,

the security blanket
you were wrapped in
at the hospital
the day you were born—
a tattered rag
in the pile of cleaning supplies—

the lines of teddy bears
on the shelves
at the Salvation Army store,
reeking of the scent
of having once been loved
but now forgotten.

I
am
so easy
to
leave
behind.

MOONSET

The fact of the moon
is that it is maybe the loneliest of us all—
only seen because of the sun,
only seen when we are at our darkest.

I wish I had been your sun,
instead of your moon,
some glow that got you through a dark night or two
that you've already forgotten now it's day,
that you can't even acknowledge
when I ask if you're still fine.

You said you always found yourself unloved,
but what you really meant
was love comes from the wrong places,
so my love didn't count.
This is something I have
gradually
begun to adjust to,
as each passing year
seems to see me become
a little less valid
in the eyes of the men
I want to adore—
the men who only see
the extra years,
the extra pounds,
the thin streaks of grey.
But it's never been just that,
has it?

Every deep passion I have ever felt
has been directed to a black hole
that reflected none of it back.
I am always what was not meant.
I am always too much assumed.
I am always
one night, when he didn't mean to go so far.
When I open myself to allow passion,
to rise toward what at first seems
like true romantic need,
it always becomes a signal broadcast
into empty space,
like radio frequencies
reaching out toward the stars.

My love mingles in galaxies
with top 40 hits
from 1990,
my first true love,
his eyes so blue,
never staring back at me,
only through,
somehow, I guess,
much like you.

Except you saw even less
than he ever did,
because you never really tried.

It's pointless to hate you, really.
Almost as pointless as loving you,
since in the end, you're not there
to feel any of what I do.
In the end, what do I have to offer?
I can't even mourn you
with a decent poem.

ACKNOWLEDGEMENTS

First and foremost, special thanks to the following publications which have featured or will soon feature some of the poems contained in this book (occasionally in slightly different form):

Animal: A Beast of a Literary Magazine ("Distemper"), *Assaracus* ("Scarification," "Romance Novels," "Consider the Moon"), *Black River Review* ("Missed Connections," "The Lycanthrope's Dream"), *Lips* ("Bonds"), *MiPOesias* ("Police Line"), *OCHO* ("Soma Cube," "The New Mattress"), *Paterson Literary Review* ("Drink of Water"), and *Sugar Mule* ("How I Lost My Vanilla Ice T-Shirt"). Each of these magazines puts a great deal of time and effort into discovering and revealing fresh new voices, and I wouldn't be doing any of this without their efforts. Please check them out and see the wonderful work they do.

Maria Mazziotti Gillan, my teacher and mentor. If it were not for you, I would not be writing poetry. I would still be struggling to pretend I was a novelist despite never having finished a novel, and all of the things that have been poured into these poems would still be locked inside of me, keeping me up at night. There is no better teacher a beginning poet could ask for, and I am proud to think of you as My Mother of Poetry.

Bryan Borland at Assaracus and Sibling Rivalry Press, who was the first person to ever publish any of my poems, and accepted not just one but ten! The boundless energy you put into your work, the beauty you discover and print so the world can see it, and the time and effort you put into building not just a publishing house but a family are incredible gifts that you give to the world.

Ann Clark, Christie Grimes, and Stacy Pratt—sisters in poetry and each an amazing writer in their own right. Each of you has given me inspiration and strength to not only start on but continue with this journey. This book and Jane's Boy are as much a piece of you as it is a piece of me.

Finally, to the people I have worked with in workshops and classrooms over the last five years. I truly believe there is an energy that comes into a room full of people engaged in the process of creation. It is always a pleasure to work with a group of people focused on finding the hard truth and putting it into words. Write on!

I always hate writing these things, because I'm sure I am leaving someone out who should be here. If that someone is you, know that the sin is of my failing memory, not of my true heart.

And thank you to you, Dear Reader. Keep poetry alive by spreading it to other people and showing them it is so much more than what they may think of what they were sold in moldy textbooks in public school classrooms. Poetry is alive and well and vital to the human condition. Jane's Boy Press will continue to do its part to spread the word, but your help makes a bigger impact than we can all alone. Share the words you love with the people you love.

JANE'S BOY PRESS

Thank you for buying this Jane's Boy book. The mission of Jane's Boy is to help new, emerging, and established poets reach new audiences. We believe that poetry is alive and well and essential to the day-to-day lives that we lead. We seek to publish diverse voices that bring that insistent vitality to the fore of their work. Please visit our website to learn more about our press, our mission, our authors, and our future projects. Better yet, consider letting your voice be a part of the movement, and submit something to our manuscript review process or for our print journal. Don't let yourself be one of those voices that goes unheard because the best of what you have to say is locked in old notebooks hidden in attic boxes or shoved inside a dresser drawer. Share what you have to say with us, and we may be able to help you share it with the world.

www.janesboypress.com

www.ingramcontent.com/pod-product-compliance
Lightning Source LLC
Chambersburg PA
CBHW061756040426
42447CB00011B/2322